Truffles
FROM
Heaven

DISCOVERING THE SWEET
GIFT OF GOD'S GRACE

Kali Schnieders

Chariot Victor Publishing
A Division of Cook Communications

Chariot Victor Publishing,
Cook Communications, Colorado Springs, Colorado 80918
Cook Communications, Paris, Ontario
Kingsway Communications, Eastbourne, England

TRUFFLES FROM HEAVEN
© 1999 by Kali Schnieders
Printed in Singapore
Editors: Becky Freeman, Lee Hough
Design: Big Cat Marketing Communications
Photography: Don Jones Photography

Unless otherwise noted, all Scripture quotations are from the *New American Standard Bible (NASB)*, © the Lockman Foundation 1960, 1962, 1963, 1968, 1971, 1972, 1973, 1975, 1977. Other references are from the *Revised Standard Version of the Bible* (RSV), © 1946, 1952, 1971, 1973; *The Living Bible* (TLB), © 1971, Tyndale House Publishers, Wheaton, IL 60189. Used by permission.

1 2 3 4 5 6 7 8 9 10 Printing/Year 03 02 01 00 99

Library of Congress Cataloging-in-Publication Data
Schnieders, Kali
        Truffles from heaven: discovering the sweet gift of God's grace/Kali Schnieders.
        p.   cm.
    Includes bibliographical references.
    ISBN   1-56476-764-7
    1. Christian life.   I. Title.
    BV4501.2.S2965   1999   99-28092
    242--dc21   CIP

This book is dedicated to the glory of God,
and to the memory of my parents.

With love to Larry and Elizabeth,
with gratitude to my editors,
Becky Freeman and Lee Hough,
and with appreciation to each friend
who prayed this book into completion.

You are my treasured truffles.

Acknowledgments

Candygram Truffles

George Matheson, "O Love That Will Not Let Me Go."

Truffles and Beaus

Ellen Burstyn, as quoted in *Courage to Change* (New York: Al-Anon Family Group Headquarters, Inc., 1992).

Unspoken Truffle

Phyllis Diller, as quoted in *1,911 Best Things Anybody Ever Said,* Robert Byrne (New York: Ballantine Books, 1988).

Penny Candy...

Frederick Buechner, *Telling Secrets*, as quoted in *Spiritual Literacy*, Frederick and Mary Ann Brussat (New York: Scribner, 1996).

Contents

What's a Truffle from Heaven, Anyway?....1

Heavenly Truffles in Bittersweet Times.........6

Candygram Truffle...............................17

Truffles and Beaus...............................28

My White-Chocolate-Truffled Knight.......44

Trousseau of Truffles............................52

Unspoken Truffle.................................60

The Truffle with Cookies........................69

Truffled Feathers.................................77

Key Lime Truffles................................85

Friendship Truffles..............................91

Penny Candy or Truffle Treasure?.............98

Speaking of Truffles............................108

Truffled Reunion................................116

What's a Truffle from Heaven, Anyway?

*"Life is like a box of chocolates.
You never know what you're gonna get."*

Forrest Gump

*F*orrest's mama was right. Perhaps today life will offer you some great thrill—a newfound friend, a marriage proposal, the birth of a child, or an exciting new job. Or maybe what will come out of the box is an assortment of heartache: sudden, irreversible, the kind that forever changes the way you live and relate to others. Wherever you find yourself at the end of the day, whatever the mix of life's unexpected ups and downs you may experience, you can always, always count on each day containing truffles from heaven.

Chocolate lovers know truffles are small, gourmet delights, often a gift between lovers. A truffle from heaven is also a gift between lovers. "God, being rich in mercy, because of His great love with which He loved us"[1] knocks on our doors daily, offering truffles of hope and encouragement, comfort and love.

Our part is to slow down, pause long enough to recognize and receive the truffles God sends in a very personal, usually unobtrusive way.

I remember once during a time of great grief, I came home to find a surprise on my doorstep. I opened the paper sack to discover all of the makings for seven-bean soup: seven different kinds of beans, an onion, a can of diced tomatoes, spices (premeasured and sealed in a small zipper bag), and a tiny bottle of hot pepper sauce.

A beautiful card tucked inside the bag read:

> *I know this is a difficult time for you. Your sadness must be overwhelming. I've found that it sometimes brightens my day just to have a fresh, piping hot pot of soup cooking on the stove. Even when I don't have an appetite—the aroma gives me a spiritual lift I*

---

[1] Ephesians 2:4

cannot describe. I cook, God listens. For that reason I didn't cook the soup myself. I wanted you to have the day-long joy of the aroma and a cooking chat with the Lord.

Love, Diane

The tenderness represented by that heavenly bag of groceries touched me deeply.

I indulged my soul with a good cry, then wiped away my tears, set the card in my kitchen window, and began to chop the onion. Though my circumstances hadn't changed, my burden was somehow lighter. And it wasn't simply that I received food on my doorstep, it was seeing beyond that and recognizing God at work, through others, to let me know that He cared, He understood the pain. That's all I needed, and I was ready to face the next few hours with grace.

If you've been a Christian for any length of time, you know that God doesn't typically come flying into a crisis with Superman news, "Here I am to save the day!" But He does come with paper sacks full of tenderness, and He's always ready to listen while we cook. Perhaps you, too, can remember a small gesture of kindness that enabled you to hold on and hang in during a hard time.

Unfortunately, receiving heaven's truffles doesn't come naturally to most of us. It is a way of seeing and hearing with a heightened spiritual awareness that must be cultivated. The good news is that, if we are willing, we can develop such a spiritual sensitivity in the everyday moments of life.

Truffles from heaven arrive in all shapes, sizes, colors, and flavors. Sometimes the truffle comes in the form of a person, divinely placed in our life at a critical moment. Other times it may be given in a penetrating verse of Scripture that captures our present situation in an intimate, uncanny way, as though it were written just for us. Occasionally it is material, like a favorite flavor of yogurt.

Whatever the size or shape of the truffle, all these heavenly gifts share this in common: They originate with God, not with us. They cannot be conjured up. They arrive; choice gifts personally selected from the riches of His grace and gently placed in the palm of your life. Every truffle has its own unique nougat center message from God. The work of life is to get that message.

This collection of stories represents God's gift box of choice truffles given to me during times when I needed to sense His presence and comfort. It is my heartfelt prayer that you will be encouraged to find the divinely placed truffles in your own life. And to know that He loves you.

Nougat Center

*O taste and see
that the Lord is good.*

(Ps. 34:8)

Heavenly Truffles
in Bittersweet Times

*R*eflecting on my early years, I find my childhood faith was strong, but as with most children, I was short on wisdom. I just wanted to be loved and admired. Instead of turning my heart toward heaven for acceptance, I aimed my little eyes toward Atlantic City. From the time I was five years old, I joined the throngs of girls worshipping at the altar of the great American beauty pageant, thinking, *If only I could be good enough to wear a crown, I'd really be SOMEBODY.*

And then, my wish came true.

At the age of twenty-one, I became the reigning Miss Missouri World. Ultimately I competed in a most memorable pageant—Miss World USA. I stood alongside forty-nine very beautiful women that night, but the most stunning (and, of course, the proclaimed winner) was Miss Arizona. You may be familiar with her name, Linda Carter, or her famous television role—*Wonder Woman.*

Today as I speak around the country, I'm always amused by the expressions in the audience when I mention that little tidbit about *Wonder Woman*. It's as though people expect ME to look like Linda Carter, but it's clear to everyone that the sand in my hourglass certainly doesn't reflect the standard beauty queen measurements of "36-24-36."

My figure looks much more like a long, thin balloon that has been squeezed disproportionately leaving a dramatic crimp in the middle, a bulb at the bottom, and barely a blossom at the top.

As a preteen girl I was anything but pleased with my flat chest. So I decided to give God a helping hand. I madly wanted to impress a thirteen-year-old neighbor and heartthrob named Steve, so I stuffed several four-inch-square carpet samples (they'd previously served as throw rugs for my Barbie doll) into the top of my bikini. I remember gazing in the mirror, admiring the voluptuous illusion I'd ingeniously created.

However, the instant I took my first plunge into

the pool, the carpet squares dislodged from my swimsuit top and immediately rose to the surface of the water. My glorious figure simply floated away. Needless to say, I was horrified. If I drew Steve's attention, it certainly wasn't with my figure. But if Swimming-in-Pursuit-of-Carpet-Squares could have been an Olympic event, the record I set in that August afternoon of 1963 would have been impressive.

When I share these stories, women naturally want to know, "If you are not 'beauty pageant material,' Kali, then why did you enter the contests?"

The answer doesn't come easy, even now, after years of reflection. I know that when my father left our home and quickly remarried, my child-sized heart broke in two and my mother's heart seemed shattered beyond repair. Though Dad moved out before I celebrated my ninth birthday, the trauma of his absence sent shock waves vibrating into my adolescence and beyond.

My father's departure from our family left me feeling like a sheet of stationery, monogrammed with his initials, then wadded up and cast into the trash can. For all his good qualities, my father was never fond of children, or of expressing his feelings. How I longed to hear my father's voice say the words, "I love you," or even "I think you're pretty." But mostly I yearned to hear Dad say, "I'm proud of you. I'm glad you're my daughter just the way you are."

In a desperate search for Dad's approval, I determined to excel in an area that seemed to have captured his fascination—beautiful women. Even though my father never attended any of my pageants, I focused on the notion that if I could convince a panel of judges to declare through their votes, "Hey, now here's a pretty and talented girl," then I might believe it myself.

I surmised that even if my dad never expressed his love, a glance at my crown would remind me that one wonderful day, twelve people found me to be worthy of notice. Then I'd know, really know, that I would be deserving of a good man's love somewhere, someday. So the glittering crown was, to me, the coveted prize of being valued—and I determined to work as hard as I could for that rhinestone headdress of self-worth.

It would be no easy task. My transition from childhood to womanhood was certainly far from glamorous.

I'll never forget the first day of seventh grade as I

watched the other girls get off the school bus wearing dyed-to-match pleated skirts and mohair sweaters, hose, and Cappezio shoes! Meanwhile, I shuffled onto the stage of junior high dressed by my mother in a multitude of petticoats under a full, circular skirt, wearing the same white, lacy anklets and patent leather shoes that had become my elementary school trademark.

"Nonsense," my mother retorted when I begged for a pair of hose that afternoon. "At your age? I can't afford to buy you hose. You'll run a new pair every day. Besides, you look so cute in anklets."

After her divorce, it was as if my mother felt compelled to slam on the brakes of her daughter's development in order to keep all four wheels on solid pavement as long as possible.

"Then at least let me shave my legs!" I begged, my high-pitched whine revealing my desperation.

"Now don't keep pestering me about shaving your legs. Why, your hair is so light it's barely noticeable," Mom countered.

But the twelve-year-old popularity mavens had noticed my hairy legs, and this faux pas, combined with my babyish clothes, had already placed my "in-crowd" status in serious jeopardy.

Sixth grade had been so easy. My fashion sense had been up to par, and my popularity a general source of comfort. Now nothing about school was comforting. There were male teachers barking orders in the hall! (I thought all teachers were supposed to wear kindly smiles and skirts.) No longer could I count on staying snugly tucked into my classroom for the entire day. I had to find seven different rooms, and all before the bell rang. I dared not imagine what might happen if I was unable to locate my classes before the bell.

But by far the most horrifying adjustment of all was gym class. First, I was no athlete. The most sportsy thing I'd done to this point was put a swimsuit on my Barbie doll. My stomach churned when I learned we'd have to "dress out" in a loathsome blue uniform, which my mother, of course, starched into a cardboardlike crispness. Also, to my everlasting shame, Mom embroidered my name on the pocket!

Around the corner from the gymnasium sat the mother lode of my pubescent fears: the shower stalls. There I would face the most shocking adjustment of all. I'd have to parade naked in front of other female classmates. No mere carpet square could save me now.

My hair was my sole hope of salvation that year. In the hair arena, I blended in with my peers, sporting the ever-popular, shoulder-length, 1960s "bare flip" (worn by Shelley Fabares on *The Donna Reed Show*). I counted on that flip as my ticket to acceptance by Dottie Smith and Leslie Mills,[1] the movers and shakers of Antioch Junior High.

The power that Dottie and Leslie wielded was enormous, carrying my fragile self-worth around each day on the tips of their tongues. One word and I could be banished from the in-crowd forever; a smile from their lips in my direction, and I'd be welcomed in at least for the day. Grade school had not prepared me for the unspoken Law of Junior High Popularity: The in-crowd giveth, and the in-crowd taketh away.

I breathed a sigh of relief that first week of school when I discovered that Dottie and Leslie also sported bare flips, knowing at least my hairstyle would receive a blessing from the reigning teenage goddesses.

About that same time, my dear Aunt Fran graduated from beautician school and opened her own shop. Aunt Fran was always generous with Mom and me, often buying my school clothes and essentials when

---

[1]Names have been changed.

the stress of our financial worries became too much for us to handle. Since the weighty price of a perm would ordinarily have been more than our budget could bear, Aunt Fran offered to give us each a free cut and perm. Mom hopped on this opportunity to travel first class and my hair was along for the ride.

Upon close examination of my current hairdo, Aunt Fran explained to Mom, "See, Betty. Kali's long, straight style elongates her face. It doesn't properly set off her high cheekbones." Yada, yada, yada. They chattered on like two women at a fruit market, poking my head as if they were examining a melon on sale. Never once did my objections receive more than a brief acknowledgment.

Before I even knew what had buzzed by my head, my bare flip was lying on the floor of Fran's House of Beauty. And with it fell my only sure popularity ticket. By the time the clipping, perming, and teasing was complete, I swiveled around in the beauty chair to face the mirror and the facts: I looked exactly like Folly, our French poodle. Hot tears fell down my cheeks, as every hope I'd cherished of being friends with Dottie and Leslie was swept into a dustpan and emptied into the trash. (To this day I still interview potential stylists with the question, "Have you ever, at any time in your professional career, produced a hairdo even remotely resembling a poodle?")

But my nightmares in seventh grade were not limited to hair troubles. Mom also enrolled me in Speech I, convinced the class would help me overcome my shyness. I dreaded the moment I'd be forced to stand up, speak out, and be noticed, particularly by my instructor, Mr. Shipp. Each day Mr. Shipp strode into class with the confidence of a politician running for office unopposed. He was also . . . rather easy on the eye.

Great, I thought. *Where are those sweet little grandmotherly teachers when a girl really needs 'em?*

When the time finally came for my first speech, I gasped as I read: You shall perform the poem by James Thurber entitled "Excelsior." I'm not certain what Thurber hoped to communicate in those verses; I only know that at various moments the poem seemed to require a loud, dramatic calling out of the word EXCELSIOR! This I accomplished with a gust of volume and a solitary finger pointed heavenward (from whence I hoped my help would come).

Between stanzas my breathing could be heard as

actual, audible gasps. My hands clasped the poem so tightly, and quivered so rapidly, the paper vibrated. This contributed a fluttering sound to my reading (and I do mean reading). I began to perspire like Grandpa's forehead after a bowl of Grandma's chili. I made little (if any) eye contact, and stumbled over my own feet as I stepped away from the podium.

I lowered my head when Mr. Shipp approached with my evaluation. I couldn't look at him or read the slip of paper for fear I'd burst into tears. When the bell rang, I dashed from the room to read Mr. Shipp's remarks in private.

There at the top of the page in red ink, Mr. Shipp had forcefully written my grade. I was amazed. Three simple lines on a white piece of paper, formed the letter A. Those three small lines were followed by three HUGE words that changed my life: *Good job, Kali.*

Mr. Shipp must have heard a whisper from the lips of God. "All the child needs is encouragement!"

Speech became my favorite subject, and my fear of male instructors was brushed aside with every stroke from Mr. Shipp's red pen. I received an A for every speech I gave. Unknowingly, Mr. Shipp was helping to steer the course of my life. Today I am a professional speaker, delivering messages about God's love and His truffles of grace and hope. Occasionally I glance over my shoulder at bygone years and smile as I notice the footprints of the Almighty—His planning so careful, the details so precious. Even through the awkward years, when I thought my life was doomed by bad hair, carpet squares, and terminal shyness, God sent truffles of encouragement when I needed them most.

Nougat Center

For I know the plans I have for you, says the Lord, plans for welfare and not for evil, to give you a future and hope.

(Jer. 29:11 RSV)

Candygram Truffle

A treasured friend recently shared with me his newfound affection for the Lord's Prayer. For more than twenty years he recited it as many do, by rote. Today he speaks as one who has had an inner spark rekindled: "'Give me this day my daily bread.' That daily bread is God Himself. What I want, what we all want, more than material things is the life-giving sacrament of His love, His presence. When I say the Lord's Prayer now, it's in a whole new way. I'm asking for, and opening my heart to receive the Bread of Life—Christ."

As I listened to my friend share, I understood exactly what he meant. I, too, want to receive a portion of God each day. Call it bread, manna, or truffles, every day I need it, I need Him, something solid, substance for the soul.

But will we receive Him? Will we notice the Bread when it is given in the rush of the day? Just as the wise men found the Savior lying in an obscure manger, truffles are often uncovered in places where we'd least expect to find them. If we have eyes that see.

For me, it helps to begin my day in prayer, "Lord, I know You will be talking to me in a million different ways. And You know what a distracted wanderer I can be, so help me to see every blessing, seize every joy You planned today before I ever drew a breath. I don't want to miss Your treasure in my humdrum day. Help me to recognize every small sacrament coming from heaven. Open my spirit to the nourishment You offer. I need my daily bread today, and I thank You for it in advance."

I wish I could tell you I always prayed to discover heavenly truffles in the everyday, but I can't. I lived for many years lost in what I now call the "black hole," and worst of all, I was in too deep to realize I'd slipped into an abyss. How well I remember the night my rescue from darkness began. I sat on the sofa, mindlessly spooning a bowl of noodle soup into my mouth, while my best friend, Pandy (the wonder dog!), leaned against my leg. I clicked the television remote, from one humorless sitcom to another. *So this is my big celebration,* I thought. Two hours ago I'd received the largest order in my nine-year sales career. I'd just unseated my arch rival and strongest competitor from the most coveted account in my territory. No one (including me) thought I could pull this off. Unlike David, who felled his foe with one well-placed rock, I fought for three years using every weapon in our corporate arsenal to bring down my giant. Finally victory was mine!

Instead of cheering, however, I was weeping. I would have loved to spend the evening sipping champagne from my shoe, tossing it in the fire, dancing 'round the room in the arms of a loving man. I wanted to feel the jubilation of my success. In truth, what I really longed to do was to share the moment. *With a husband by my side,* I mused, *even canned soup might seem like a feast.*

I thought over the advice my mother had given me about surviving, being independent, making sure I'd never be enslaved to a man financially. I'd followed her advice, convinced it would guarantee happiness and freedom. What I hadn't realized was that Mom's counsel about romance had come from an emotionally scarred heart.

After Dad left us, she'd been abruptly thrust into the workforce. With only a high school diploma and no work experience, Mom was ill-equipped and unprepared to face our financial reality. We'd been financially secure; now paying basic bills would be a constant struggle. Mom's greatest concern was for my education (one additional reason for my entering the pageants—they offered college scholarships). Frequently she said, "I don't care if I have to scrub floors to pay for it, you're going to college." She meant it.

And now many years later, my college diploma in hand, good fortune in the world of business had produced for me some measure of financial independence. In this area, Mom had prepared me well. But I was woefully unprepared for the feeling of loneliness within my heart this particular night. Even as I saw my corporate star rising to a great new height, I felt my spirit sinking to an even greater low point. I had no mate with whom to share my joy—or my sorrow.

"What's wrong with me, Pandy?" I asked the only living thing nearby. "Why did God put this desire in my heart for a mate, if He won't provide one?"

I carried on my pitiful conversation with a black-and-white ball of fluff, never voicing my question directly to God. Maybe I didn't want to know why as much as I wanted a husband, and *now.* I hungered for cozy evenings, snuggling with a mate in front of the fireplace. Like a wedding ring on a string, the image of matrimonial togetherness dangled ever before me.

Moonlight streamed in the picture window of my family room, while I took inventory of myself for the zillionth time: I had above average intelligence, a ready sense of humor, and reasonably good looks. I was respected by my customers and peers at work, and I earned a decent income. I kept myself physically fit, had interesting hobbies, wonderful friends, and I loved animals!

"I'm starting to sound like a poster child for the Girl Scouts." Pandy cocked his head at my exasperated tone of voice, then he scratched his ear. *I'd better get a grip,* I thought. *I'm pouring out my heart to a French poodle as though he's a two-hundred-dollar-an-hour psychotherapist. Worse yet, I'm expecting answers!*

Momentarily, I stopped addressing the dog and

tossed out my next lament to the great Someone out there. "So what's wrong with me?" I questioned silently, feeling like the passed over child in a playground game. To which God probably replied, "You're not ready yet." But I never heard Him. For I was mostly venting and whining this particular night; I hadn't learned about listening.

The next morning I hurried off to my Sunday School class, grumbling to myself about the rain. The parking lot of my beloved Village Church, tucked in the heart of Mission, Kansas, was crowded. Rain, of course, always increased the parishioners' incentives to park nearby, so my mood spiraled downhill from grumbling to outright disgust. I finally found a parking place within hiking distance. As a single woman, I always strived to look my best on Sunday—just in case.

"Today Mr. Magnificent will probably sit next to me," I complained under my breath, "and I'll look like a wet alley cat." Slipping into my seat, I wiped the rain from the back of my legs and struggled to come up with a positive thought.

Class began in the usual way, a short time of fellowship followed by prayer and a lesson. I knew this Sunday the message might be intriguing because we had a guest speaker; I had no idea it would be life changing. The speaker began by saying, "I brought a letter for you," and we were each instructed to slip our own name into the salutation. Not easily manipulated, I ordinarily would have just listened politely, guarding emotions too near my heart. But for some inexplicable reason I played along, listening as though someone was reading me a letter from a dear friend.

The letter perfectly described an average day in my life, and the message penetrated deep to a place in my spirit I didn't know existed. Like a verbal massage, the news felt like tender fingers, skillfully stroking my weary heart. But then the healing words also began pressing on some sore spots.

The letter expressed great care for me, as though my daily steps were being traced by Love itself. The Writer described viewing me at a distance, as I walked with my friends, hoping for an invitation to join in. I felt a pang of guilt as I imagined His hurt at being left out of the in-circle of my life.

The Writer spoke of watching my day turn sour, of how He longed to reach out and comfort me. (At this point, I started to squirm.) In one last attempt to gain my attention, to encourage me to make a new start, the Writer of the letter, who said He was my Friend, sent a gift—a rainbow across the sky. The letter was signed, "I love you, Jesus."

A physical pain gripped at me, and for a few moments I fought for composure. Me, the calm, cool, businesswoman, undone by a sentimental letter! I'll never know how other class members reacted. I suspect some of them tossed it off, as I might have done at another time, a piece too emotional to be taken seriously. But I was at what psychologists call "a point of felt need"—my armor gone, my vulnerability exposed. The thought that God was personally interested in me touched my need for love and acceptance deeply, and suddenly I felt terribly ashamed that I'd not recognized before the signs of His love.

What if it's true? I dared to ask, as I walked out of the church to my car. I looked up. Even through the tears I could trace the outline—a rainbow shimmered in the sky. The lyrics of a favorite hymn played in my ears, "I trace the rainbow through the rain, and feel the promise is not vain, that morn shall tearless be." The image was haunting. *What if I'm not alone after all?*

All day and into the night questions tugged at my spirit. "Dare I believe God loves me this much? That He wants to be that intimate? What if He really did send beautiful little love gifts into my day with intentions of comfort and reassurance?" In the absence of a husband who might bring me chocolates, was God sending me heavenly truffles each day? And if He was, I not only failed to thank Him for His gifts, I failed even to notice them.

"Lord," I prayed, this time as if to a good friend, "I've stiff-armed happiness most of my life, haven't I? I keep refusing to simply let it in." I'd unconsciously made up my mantra, *I will be happy when* . . . filling in the blank with a multitude of desires. The list loomed long. *When I graduate. When I find the right job . . . the right man. When I make that sale . . .* Most of us, if we're honest, have lists that keep happiness at bay.

The memory of the letter and the rainbow that followed lingered into the evening. As I was getting ready for bed, my mood was heavy. I couldn't stop thinking about my restlessness, my lonely life. I couldn't face the ten o'clock news, with all its unsettling stories, not tonight.

Before I lie down to sleep, I thought, *I need a*

reason to get up in the morning. I reached for the old, worn Bible I'd received when I was a little girl of nine. Allowing the pages to part and fall open at will, my eyes rested in Isaiah. For the second time in one day, tears came, wetting the pages as I read, "For your Maker is your husband . . . the God of the whole earth he is called. For the Lord has called you like a wife forsaken and grieved in spirit . . ." (Isa. 54:5-6 RSV).

How often I'd read Isaiah, never noticing this particular verse. "I'm taking You up on that promise, Lord," I whispered, turning out the light and pulling Pandy close. "I'll gladly take You to be my husband, if You can put up with me as Your bride." I felt more peace than I'd known in many years.

In the morning my circumstances hadn't changed at all, but my pessimistic approach to living was about to topple. That promise from the Lord was a lifeline out of my black hole. The strength in my voice surprised me. Battling my old habits, and fighting off depressing thoughts, I spoke aloud new truth to my own ears. "The Lord is my Husband, the Lover of my soul, and the Lifter of my head. I can share every joy and sorrow with Him, just as I would a mate."

When I meet women who are single, never married, divorced, or widowed, I love to share with them the comfort found in that verse from Isaiah. And when God asks each of us—married or single— "Do you take Me as your mate? Will you walk with Me day to day, in sickness and in health?" May we all respond with uninhibited joy and reverence, "I do— oh, yes, Jesus, I do."

Nougat Center

Whom have I in heaven but Thee?
And besides Thee,
I desire nothing on earth.
My flesh and my heart may fail;
But God is the strength of my heart
and my portion forever.

(Ps. 73:25-26)

Truffles and Beaus

What a lovely surprise to discover how un-lonely being alone can be." This discovery by Ellen Burstyn aptly described my attitude toward being single in the late 1980s. In the months following my decision to trust God to be my nearest companion, even to be the Husband of my heart, my former anxiety over finding an earthly mate vanished. No longer did I feel the intense vacuum of loneliness. I wasn't dead set against marriage; it was just no longer a requirement for my contentment.

Nearly fifteen years earlier, when my brief, three-year marriage ended in divorce, I was not only brokenhearted, I was forced to admit to myself and to God that the failure fell largely on my own shoulders. I had a strange reaction to the guilt over the failure of my marriage. A woman, if she's wise, will approach new relationships with extra caution if her first marriage ends. But I felt I had something to prove— mostly to myself. I believed I could have a successful marriage; I just needed to find the right partner.

For several years immediately following my divorce, I approached dating like a reckless gambler spooning quarters into a slot machine. "If I just keep putting my heart into the effort and pulling the handle, sooner or later I'll hit the jackpot," I told myself. But the wheel of fortune in my relationships not only failed to turn up "cherries"—it consistently turned up lemons. I was so blind, it never occurred to me that I might be a lemon myself.

It has been said that marriage is our last, best chance to grow up. Sadly, my marriage and divorce had not produced an adult. But now my walk with God was closer, and I had begun to learn some valuable lessons. I realized my finding the right person to marry was not so important to God. My *becoming* the right person, married or single, meant everything to Him. Once I became a willing lump of clay, God was pleased to mold me.

Once I focused on becoming a vessel of God's love (instead of how I could find a husband), I began to like and love the woman God was re-creating me to be. I feared that adding a mate to the mix might actually distract me from my new, more spiritual focus.

After admitting that my first marriage had not been based on the highest of principles, I decided if I were to ever marry again, I'd need more discernment in the selection process. So with a pen in my hand, and a prayer on my lips, I composed a list of characteristics I wanted in a mate.

I wrote down things like:

1. A strong faith
2. A positive outlook
3. Commitment for life
4. Honesty, integrity . . .

I tucked the white slip of paper into my Bible and prayed, "Lord, this is a man with whom I could happily spend the rest of my life. If You have one like this, and it's Your will for me to remarry, I'm willing. The choice is Yours. I only ask You to help me know him when I see him. If he never shows up, I'll be content to live out my days on earth with You as my companion."

☙

I was irritated by the ringing of the telephone.

"Who in the world is calling in the middle of the ten o'clock news?" I grumbled aloud. "Don't these people ever stop working? I should just let the machine take over . . ."

Since 1984 I'd enjoyed having my office in my home, but the arrangement occasionally had its disadvantages. Clients called at all hours, and I felt compelled to respond. Not tonight, though. I was determined to give my over-developed sense of responsibility a rest. Yet for some unexplained reason, I responded to an inner prompting to answer *this call,* even after having ignored the last three.

"Hello," I said, trying not to reveal my aggravation.

"Hi Kali, this is a voice from the past."

Who in the world is this? I wondered. The voice was so familiar, yet I was momentarily stumped.

"It's Larry."

"No kidding! I don't believe it! How are you?" I squealed.

I knew Larry from my college days at Central Missouri State University. He was smart, funny, and we shared many common interests. I thought the world of him, but since I had another boyfriend, our relationship remained light and casual. Larry had never complained about my lack of availability on the weekends, so I figured he had simply considered us great friends.

Shortly after graduation, I married, but Larry and I stayed in touch through phone calls and annual catch-up notes in Christmas cards. Eventually, Larry relocated to St. Louis and married a wonderful woman. Our frequent contacts slowly faded with new directions and the passage of time.

"So what's been going on in your life?" Larry asked breezily. Our chatter was natural, as if we'd spoken last week instead of thirteen years before. I hit the highlights of the last decade of my life: career, parents, my trip to Africa. I saved the most unpleasant subject for last. "Did you hear about my divorce?"

"Yes," Larry replied thoughtfully, "I felt bad for you." His voice turned melancholy as he shared the tragic headline from his life's news. "My wife, Annette, died two years ago."

Overwhelmed at the thought of such a loss, I fumbled for the right words, some appropriate sentiment. I found none and blathered something inadequate instead. Then Larry revealed more of the shattering circumstances surrounding Annette's tragic death. Though she'd been to a doctor for her regular checkup, the physician hadn't uncovered the serious situation developing with her heart. When Annette collapsed of heart failure, so unexpectedly, it left Larry and all who knew her reeling from shock. "But I have a little daughter, Elizabeth, who's five years old and the joy of my life," Larry concluded.

Switching to a lighter subject, Larry detailed his hopscotch moves across the country for the sake of his career. I was impressed to hear he was still with the telephone company (his first job out of college). By now, I'd worked for several different companies, and was in my sixth career move. Such loyalty was rare in the present business climate. Our lives were so different, yet some things had remained the same—Larry was still charming, and still captivated me with his humor.

"My goodness, how did you ever find me?" I asked.

"Friends at the phone company," Larry quipped. "It would be so great to see you, Kali. I'd love to spend a few hours catching up, but this is long distance."

In all of my excitement I hadn't even thought to

ask where Larry was calling from, or what had prompted his call. "I'm currently living in Austin, Texas," Larry briefly explained. "I spent today stranded at the airport with harried Thanksgiving travelers. I've had one delayed flight after another. Sitting around the terminal, alone in a crowd with not much to do, well, my mind wandered to past holidays, family, and friends. And I thought of you. When the last flight to Washington was canceled, I drove on home, and decided, "Hey, I'll be going to K.C. soon to see my folks for Christmas. Maybe Kali would be free for lunch during the holidays. The next thing I knew, I was dialing the phone."

"Well, I have a great idea, Larry," I said. "I'm having my seventh annual Christmas Day Night party." I went on to explain that each year when the gift opening, turkey eating, and general family holiday hoopla ended on Christmas Day, I found myself feeling a little down. The post-divorce blues always hit me hardest around the holidays. I thought that perhaps some of my single friends, and a few married friends with no family in town, might be feeling the same way.

"So on Christmas night, when the festivities are normally over, I invite everyone over for a big bash.

I haven't been in a down mood ever since I started this tradition, and my friends love it!" I paused to catch my breath, then concluded, "Larry, please come. It'd be wonderful to see you."

Enthusiastically, he agreed. So it was settled. I hung up the phone, thankful I had picked up the call. Christmas Day came and went. Larry never called, and never showed up at the party. I was surprised, and a little confused, but not overly disappointed. The party was always so much fun that a few no-shows never dampened my spirits.

Another year quickly passed, and it was, once again, the week before Thanksgiving. I picked up my ringing telephone.

"Hi, it's Larry. . . . I'll be coming home for Christmas to see the folks. Thought maybe we could get together to catch up on old times."

"Perfect," I said without even discussing Larry's "no show" of the previous Christmas. Somehow it just didn't seem important. "Come to my Christmas Day Night party?"

"I'd love to," Larry said. It was settled. Christmas Day came and went. Again, Larry did not call or come to the party, and I was again surprised, and confused, but still not overly disappointed.

❧

Another year quickly passed. A week before Thanksgiving the call came once more, again Larry offered no explanation about his neglecting to come the previous Christmas. For the third time I heard the familiar words: "Hi, it's Larry . . . folks . . . Christmas . . . lunch . . ." However, there was one rather dramatic change.

"I'm no longer living in Texas," he said. "In fact, you might say I'm a distant neighbor. Elizabeth and I are living in Topeka." (Topeka, Kansas was only about an hour away from where I lived.)

But this year was different for me too. "Well, Larry, I'd love to invite you to my annual Christmas party, but it's been canceled. I had some surgery earlier this month, and my doctor won't even allow me to drive. If you'd like, maybe we could pick a spot for lunch, and my boyfriend can drop me off to meet you?"

There was a long pause. Though I didn't know it, Larry was thinking, *I've been down this boyfriend trail with Kali before.* Finally he answered, "Well, we'll see. Maybe it would be better if I got settled first."

For the first time in the nearly fifteen years since

we'd met, I detected something in Larry's voice that suggested he was irritated at my mention of a boyfriend. When we hung up the phone, I sat pondering our short conversation, trying to digest what had just taken place. Was it possible that Larry had been contemplating more than a friendship? I filed the thought away.

❧

In March the telephone rang, but this time I was the one placing the call. A secretary answered, and I giggled to myself at the thought of my college buddy being called "Mister." When Larry answered the phone I teased, "Hi, Larry, it's Miss Ball . . . Kali Ball."

"Well what a nice surprise," Larry chuckled. "How'd you find me?"

"Friends at the phone company," I quipped. Then I went on to explain the purpose of my call. "I've invited a client in Topeka to be my dinner guest here in Kansas City. She and her husband are driving up, and I wonder if you'd like to join us. I thought you might enjoy meeting some nice Topekans, and after dinner, maybe you and I can have that catch-up conversation."

"I'd be delighted," Larry said, pleased to hear he'd be part of a four-person set. The night of our first date was incredible. I'll never forget the flutter of feelings as I reached to open my front door to greet a face I'd not seen for ten years. Any concerns about the awkwardness of the moment, however, were quickly dispelled. Larry simply greeted me with a boyish grin. *I'm glad the years haven't tarnished that smile,* I mused.

Indeed, the years hadn't faded Larry's manly good looks, either. He still had the same broad shoulders, brown hair, twinkling eyes, and charming smile I remembered from when we were in our twenties. Furthermore, I was touched by his masterful adaptation to single fatherhood. Immediately the proud papa flashed a photo of his seven-year-old beauty, Elizabeth. I stood looking at Larry as if I were seeing him for the very first time, and I suppose, in many ways, I was. We had only a moment for small talk before scurrying off to the restaurant, but already I was developing a deeper admiration for my old friend.

The dinner was absolutely lovely, and our catch-up chat afterward was as warm and wonderful as any we'd shared during college. Waving good-bye as Larry drove off toward Topeka, I was especially happy I had *friends* at the phone company.

One date led to another, and soon we were getting reacquainted via late-night telephone marathons. During this time, I also had many conversations with God. I was keeping one eye on the hurdles I had mentally placed in the way of matrimony. However, Larry was leaping over the characteristics I'd scribbled and tucked between the pages of my Bible as if they were mere speed bumps. Even so, I was resistant to growing too serious, and I held my emotions in check. I had found serenity in my single life and was not willing to trade that away lightly. And instant motherhood . . . I wasn't at all sure that could be God's plan for me. Was I equipped for such a challenge?

Several months after our first date, as we kissed good-bye one Sunday night, Larry stunned me with the words, "I love you, Kali." Oddly, though I'd mentally gone over the checklist of husbandly qualities in Larry, I'd not even stopped to honestly ask myself how I felt. I'd been quite content with our long-distance relationship, keeping the deep emotions of love at bay. For the first time in my dating life, I'd stopped asking myself, "Where will this lead?"

Now the big "L" word was on the table, applying

the brake pedal to my cruise control. I didn't know how to answer. If I responded truthfully and declared my ambivalence, it would undoubtedly hurt Larry's feelings; he might even give up on me and walk out of my life for good. I definitely didn't want that to happen. Yet if I declared my love in return, it would be with an uncertain heart. In a split second I had to make a decision—I knew my response could unalterably affect our future relationship.

"Larry," I said with all sincerity, "you've really taken me by surprise here. I care for you, but love . . . well, I can't honestly say I'm quite there yet. But I must admit, my feelings for you are growing stronger. Can you give me some time to adjust to our relationship taking a more serious turn?"

There, I'd said it. No going back now. We'd either weather this or we wouldn't. In my heart I felt some fear, but also a deep satisfaction. I was determined to wait for a signal from God if a deeper relationship with Larry was His best plan for my life. The silence hung between us like a dark, heavy curtain.

Thankfully, Larry didn't call off the relationship. Though he was slightly more reserved, we continued dating pretty much as before. Then one bright, sunny day Larry invited me out for a picnic, just the two of us. We rented a boat and cruised out to a beautiful spot where we dropped anchor to swim and lounge in the sun. After our meal, when it came time to head for shore, the sun was setting, the water was shimmering, and a warm breeze wrapped around us as we sped along in the boat. An unexpected feeling of contentment settled over me. While steering the boat with one hand, Larry rested his other hand on my shoulder. When I turned to smile at him, he winked, said something funny, and laughed.

With sudden poignancy, I realized I'd come to adore that laugh. The certainty was so real it was almost physical. *I love this man.* As I snuggled into Larry's arm, I watched the sun set over the gentle waves lapping at the shoreline. With upturned face, I closed my eyes, feeling God's smile of approval. Sometimes God's truffles of affirmation come slowly, settling over our heart, layer by layer, until in one moment we instantly know, "This is right. . . ."

Overcome by emotion, I was uncharacteristically quiet as Larry drove me home. When we pulled into my driveway, Larry walked me to the door and prepared to kiss me good-bye. I pulled back a bit, wanting to express my love for him in words, before he kissed me. But our emotional signals crossed. Larry stiffened at my attempt to disentangle from his embrace, perhaps a little miffed at what he perceived to be my moodiness. Here was my big moment, and I was blowing it. Somehow rather than express my love, I'd conjured up irritation!

In exasperation I blurted out, "What I'm trying to say is . . . I love you . . . you knucklehead!" It all came out before I could rehearse it. I'd so wanted this moment to be romantic and perfect. I wanted to tell him I loved him softly, sweetly, ever so gently. But there it was. I'd just called the love of my life, the man of my dreams, God's choice for me—a knucklehead.

Breaking into that fabulous smile, Larry's eyes met mine. "I may be a knucklehead," he said, "but I'm one incredibly happy knucklehead." We laughed and embraced once more, as I mentally checked off a few more points from the list of husbandly qualities I'd prayed for:

1. He'll tolerate my craziness.

2. He'll be a *fabulous* kisser.

Nougat Center

Blessed be the Lord,
Because He has heard the voice
of my supplication.
The Lord is my strength
and my shield;
My heart trusts in Him,
and I am helped;
Therefore my heart exults.

(Ps. 28:6-7)

My White-Chocolate-Truffled Knight

I had not minded being an only child, really. At least not until 1989, when I found myself pacing in the waiting room. I'll never forget the surgeon rounding the corner in his pale green garb, pulling at the strings of his surgical mask. His gaze fixed heavenward, I could sense that he desperately wanted to avoid my pleading eyes. His expression was pure compassion as he drew a deep breath, and soberly delivered the heartbreaking news.

My mother was dead.

Death was sudden, unexpected, unthinkable. Mom had just been admitted to the hospital for a routine angioplasty. We'd been through this before. Thirty minutes into the procedure the nurse had said, "She did well, the doctor's just finishing up.

Go on downstairs and get a bite to eat."

Halfway through my hamburger, the nurse returned—something had gone terribly wrong. I dashed for the waiting room as if my mother's survival depended upon my arrival, as if my running could prevent the turn of events to follow. But I could not outrun the hideous day that would forever change my life.

With my dear Aunt Fran and Uncle Bob by my side, long tortuous hours in the waiting room began. We prayed for a word of hope. The kind nurse appeared occasionally offering medical updates. Her technical jargon confused us, but her facial expression always told the truth; the nurse's eyes became our windows into Mom's condition. It's easy to see the difference between cautious optimism and grave concern in the expression of a compassionate soul, and at different times, the nurse reflected both emotions. After each word of hope, our fervent prayers would resume.

Death continued its ping-ponging of our emotions until four hours later, when we were given the final verdict: all hope was now gone. The surgeon explained, "Her brain was deprived of oxygen for much too long; we'll need your permission to remove life support." I asked for a moment alone. I could not make this unalterable move without prayer. I sought out the empty hospital room where Mom had spent her last night on this earth—a place where I might still sense her nearness, and smell her fragrance.

Through spirit-wrenching sobs I bent my knees, remembering the last words I'd shared with Mom. "I love you. I'll be right here waiting. I'll see you in a minute." I had no way of knowing how long that "minute" would be. I bowed my head in desperation, pleading with God for some miracle, but only for a moment. Then a great release occurred, and I found myself offering a very different kind of prayer. I was given new strength, strength beyond my own flesh. My sorrowful prayer reached toward heaven (or as I think back on it now, perhaps heaven was reaching out to me).

"Lord," I cried, "You have blessed my days with my mother's love, but I must accept the truth. She doesn't belong to me, but to You. She was only on loan. Today, in Your wisdom, You are calling her back home. My heart is breaking, Lord, but I give her back to you with gratitude for the love we shared for so long. Please give me the strength to live in her absence." Now for the first time since my parents' divorce thirty years before, I felt utterly alone.

Returning home from the horror of the hospital, I sat in my dining room until midnight, numbly planning a memorial service. As an only child, the burden was enormous. All decisions were left to me, and me alone. I was dating Larry, but we hadn't yet discussed marriage. However, a widower himself, he proved to be a wonderful helper, showing me step-by-step what to do. The newspaper, the funeral arrangements, the flowers.

So much happened at once, my own grief mingled with the frantic activity of putting her things in order, and arranging a memorial service befitting her life. Like a rushing creek during a flash flood, my emotions were flowing over their banks, swirling, and threatening to take me under, unless I could find some branch to cling to for support. I grasped for Larry.

Slowly, painfully, Larry explained something my mind and heart could not accept. He told me he must be in St. Louis, instead of at my side, on the day of my mother's burial. "I'm scheduled to give a presentation to the top brass," Larry explained.

"Honey, for a mother-in-law's funeral, the company would be more understanding. If you were my wife, things would be different."

As it was, I was only a girlfriend. *Isn't the company aware that even girlfriends need an arm to lean on in times of grief?* I whimpered to myself. I begged Larry to skip the meeting, whatever the result, and come be with me. It pained him to say no, but in Larry's way of thinking, nearly twenty years with the company and his corporate future were at stake. Little did he know, the future of our relationship was also in jeopardy.

If I couldn't count on Larry to be there in my darkest hour, how valuable was our relationship? As I watched him walk out my front door, great feelings of resentment welled up inside, new deposits into my ever-growing pain. I felt abandoned by the one person I relied on, but those feelings would have to wait. Grief commanded my immediate attention.

Dawn greeted me with a heavy rainstorm. Oddly, I was grateful to God for the rain. It comforted me to imagine heaven in harmony with my grief. The day was dark and black, matching my spirit.

Upon arriving at the church, I waited with my

aunt and uncle until the last possible moment before entering the chapel. Then the music called us inside—"How Great Thou Art." My legs turned to rubber. I struggled to walk even as grief overtook me, and I turned to Aunt Fran for support. For a moment, I was confused by the look on her face. She wore a broad smile, then tenderly said, "Turn around, Kali." I turned—there stood Larry.

He walked through the door and, without a word, simply held out his arm. Together we walked to our pew. Together we spent the next hour celebrating my mother's triumphant entry into heaven. Together our hearts were grateful; she fought the good fight, she finished the race. Never more than at this moment did I understand Christ's words, "'For where two or three have gathered together in My name, there I am in their midst'" (Matt. 18:20).

Later I learned "the rest of the story." After Larry's presentation in St. Louis, the managers agreed he was more urgently needed elsewhere. (It is within God's power to move mountains and, when necessary, the hearts of corporate executives.) By the grace of God and, I'm sure, extra duty by unseen angels, permission was granted from somewhere at the top of the corporate ladder for the company jet to make one additional stop that day.

However, when the jet neared the Kansas City airport, the storm worsened. "Low clouds and fog may prevent our landing," the pilot said. "Will advise soon." The plane was within five minutes of diversion to another city when the fog simply . . . lifted.

"It was eerie," Larry explained to me later. "Finally, we were given the go-ahead to land. I got in my car, drove to the chapel, and arrived at the last minute." *Just when I needed him most,* I thought. *Oh, Yes, Lord, how great Thou art!*

As I sat on the couch listening to this miraculous story, I recalled the beautiful final moment in the movie *An Officer and a Gentleman.* The scene where Debra Winger is swept up into Richard Gere's arms. Stunning in his dress-white uniform, he carries her away from her dismal factory job, whisking her off to be his bride. The whole factory erupts in spontaneous applause. Romance at its finest.

In my mind's eye, I could imagine rows of heaven's angels applauding *my* gentleman as he walked through the chapel door. In that moment, Debra Winger had nothing on me.

Sometimes when grief overpowers us, it's hard for God to get our attention to soothe us. Now whenever I need special comfort from God, I often close my eyes and dwell for a moment on the incredible, unforgettable ending to that day's story. The day God dropped a gift of strength and encouragement from the stormy skies of heaven, in the form of one gallant man.

Nougat Center

No, I will not abandon you or leave you as orphans in the storm—I will come to you.

(John 14:18 TLB)

Trousseau of Truffles

*I*n the autumn of 1989, Larry and I announced our plans to marry. I'd waited a long time for the right man, and now, finally, all the circumstances seemed perfect. Except for one. "Why couldn't my mother have lived just one more year?" I cried to the Lord. I felt like a toddler wanting her mommy, angry that God had taken her away. "Did twelve months really make that much difference to You, Lord? Having Mom here for my wedding day would have made all the difference in the world to me. Weddings need a mother of the bride, don't they? Why did you take mine prematurely?"

I constantly pondered such questions in my heart and often asked myself, *If God works all things together for good, how did this happen?*

At least I still had my father. Larry and I excitedly approached Dad with our wedding plans. Even though I was in my late thirties, having my father's blessing on our marriage was very important to me. All the more reason why Dad's ensuing reaction left me baffled. After our grand announcement, my father said nothing. Not one word. He cleared his throat as if to speak, but instead, rose from his chair, opened the window, and started feeding the squirrels that were rummaging in the backyard bird feeder. For my *extremely* opinionated father this was strange behavior.

I sat for a while, wondering if Dad had heard us, unsure of what course to take next. Larry shot me a glance that said, "Tell him again." I repeated my words. "Dad, Larry and I are planning to get married. We'd like your blessing." Again silence. Dad rolled his tongue around in his mouth, as if searching there for just the right words. At the very worst, I had anticipated some overly protective, fatherly advice. Nothing could have prepared me for my father's remarks.

Finally, Dad closed the window, sat down in his recliner, his brow creasing with concern, and then poured out his worry. "You know I'm retired,

Mouse (his pet name for me since the day of my premature birth). I have no money for a fancy wedding."

Oh, my heavens, so that's the big problem, I thought. Larry and I never intended Dad to foot the wedding bill. We hadn't come for money—we had come to share our joy and receive a blessing. I felt more than a little let down. I was confused. I knew my father really liked Larry. After all, he'd nick-named him Ralph, an indication that my husband-to-be had passed my father's muster. I had expected Dad to celebrate, to be overjoyed by our news. Instead was this nervous pacing, this fretful, emotional grabbing of his wallet. The hurt child within me wanted to scream, "Daddy, share this joy! It's our wedding! You're the father of the *bride.*" I missed my mother more in that moment than I had since her passing. She had always reacted to happy news with enthusiasm; if she were alive, I knew this announcement would have evoked shouts of congratulations from a face glowing with love.

Although my mother, long divorced from my father, lived meagerly, she always saw special events as occasions to open her heart, as well as her purse strings. In all likelihood, Mom would have insisted on paying for my wedding gown. Of course, it wasn't the *gown* I longed for. I ached for enthusiasm, a happy heart, and the love behind such a gift. Yes . . . joy, that's what I missed most, in that awkward moment sitting in my father's anxious presence.

So even though I was aching now, I determined that when I began to shop for the gown, I'd simply pretend my mother was by my side, and immerse myself in the thrill of the hunt for the perfect dress. Within a week, I'd found two. The first gown, my mother would have loved, beautiful and lacy, but not quite my taste. The other dress, though twice as expensive, of course, was authentically *me*. Instantly, I fell in love with its simple, elegant style. Since the tab for the dress was mine, alone, I chose my personal favorite.

As sole heir and executor of Mom's estate, the bill paying and tidying of affairs had fallen to me. Then, nine months after I'd paid the last medical bill, I received a phone call from the hospital where Mom had died.

"It appears," said a voice from the accounting department, "you have overpaid your mother's bill. A check is in the mail to reimburse you." Great glory! When in the history of hospitals has this ever occurred? They were sending *me* a check? Unheard of. It may sound silly, but I watched the mailbox with anticipation. Whatever this money—Mom's money—amounted to, I planned to apply toward my wedding. The very thought made me feel somehow closer to my mother, as if she were sending a wedding gift from heaven.

When the envelope arrived, I recognized the hospital logo instantly (having opened so many similar envelopes with hefty bills tucked inside). But I slit open this envelope with gentle care, as if opening a wedding card of well wishes from my mother. My hands began to tremble. When I slid out the check, I could hardly breathe. I was holding matrimonial manna from heaven. The amount on the check was the exact price of my wedding gown. I felt the miracle in the envelope was God's way of allowing the mother of the bride to participate in her daughter's wedding, after all.

But God had one more gift to complete my heavenly trousseau. One morning, Dad called with a lunch invitation. The divorce between my parents had birthed bitterness on all fronts, distancing my father from me during my growing-up years. But now, about once a month, we'd spend a few precious hours eating "breakfast for lunch" at our favorite pancake place. Just a dad, his girl, and a Belgian waffle. Priceless moments.

This particular day we had quite a time chatting about the wedding plans. Dad loved to torment me. "I'm not wearing that penguin suit you picked out for me," he teased. "If you want me to walk you down the aisle, I'll wear my Hawaiian shirt." Only someone fully acquainted with my father's antics would understand why his statement caused me a few sleepless nights! (I shake my head every time I look at the photograph of Dad dressed in his floral shirt, walking shorts, calf-high black rubber boots, and a motorcycle helmet, bound for a lunch outing with his buddy, Bill.) When it came to wedding fashion, I wouldn't have put anything past him.

But my father had an even more frightening notion. Dad wanted to know when in the ceremony he could make his speech. My eyes widened as I realized—he wasn't kidding. Who knew what unpredictable comments might pop out of my father's mouth? In comparison, the Hawaiian shirt was beginning to sound like a *lovely* idea!

In spite of the teasing, we had fun together that

day. Dad drove me home from the restaurant, and when he pulled the car into my driveway, I kissed him good-bye, then reached for the door handle. But Dad touched my arm, wanting to say one more thing. I turned; he slipped an envelope in my hand. "This is between us, Mouse. A secret. Don't mention it to anyone; just a little something for your wedding."

Again, my hands trembled as I opened the envelope. Inside were several crisp bills—the exact amount of my wedding gown. I'd never discussed my dress with Dad. He had no idea of its cost. But God did, and with that knowing, He revealed through these moments with my earthly mother and father that I have a kind and generous heavenly Father . . . One who still enjoys springing surprises at weddings!

Nougat Center

*And I will give you
the treasures of darkness,
And hidden wealth of secret places,
In order that you may know
that it is I,
The Lord, the God of Israel,
who calls you by name.*

(Isa. 45:3)

Unspoken Truffle

*T*he big day had finally arrived. Carefully, I planned each hour of my wedding day. I allowed plenty of time to rise at my leisure, say a prayer of preparation, and then scamper off to the beauty shop for the works: manicure, pedicure, and of course, the hairdo.

A brief word concerning my problem hair. Oh, how I identify with the woman who said, "When I go to the beauty parlor, I always use the emergency entrance. Sometimes I just go for an estimate."

I am convinced the reason God gave me such troublesome hair is to bless me with an ever present reminder: I am not in control. My hair has a mind of its own, and that mind is devious. There are occasions when each strand of hair will march in lockstep unison, and arrange themselves on my head in an orderly fashion. But such moments are rare. That's why I'm a patsy for any new shampoo or conditioner promising to subdue rebellious locks. One particular hair-care purchase buoyed my hopes: an irresistible, antioxidant-infused conditioner laced with sea mud, and topped with avocado paste. For a while, I didn't know whether to put it on my tangled hair or my cucumber salad.

Unfortunately, the morning of my wedding was a bad hair day. Strands were spinning off, willy-nilly. *Not to worry,* I told myself, *you have Tom!* Oh, Tom . . . the mere mention of his name makes me throw both arms in the air, bend at the waist, and chant, "I'm not worthy." Tom, the lion tamer of hair follicles, has a way of making even *my* mane do his bidding.

Before the wedding, Tom and I agreed to conduct a hair rehearsal. When I arrived at the salon, wedding veil in hand, Tom was all raves. He loved designing special hairdos for brides. After a flurry of mousse and brushes, I looked in the mirror and gasped. Tom had created a masterpiece. With the majestic flare of a symphony conductor, Tom had orchestrated my wispy strands into, voilà, a masterpiece of hair harmony. "Marvelous!" he exclaimed. I couldn't have agreed more!

From that day forward, I respectfully referred to Tom as *the maestro,* trusting he would be up to a repeat performance on my wedding day. With visions of my soon-to-be glorious hair in mind, I was uncharacteristically calm during the drive to the salon. A beautiful snowfall that morning added to my sense of ethereal peace.

Pulling into the salon parking lot, veil in hand, I fairly floated in the door and greeted Connie, the receptionist, with a cheery, "Hi, I'm Kali. I'm here for my hair appointment with Tom."

Connie looked at my veil and glanced nervously around the crowded reception room. After taking a very deep breath, she leaned close to me and whispered, "I'm afraid Tom no longer works here."

I smiled. Then I calmly leaned closer to the receptionist, and in a not-so-hushed voice said, "Maybe you misunderstood me, Connie. I'm not talking about the Tom who no longer works here; I'm talking about the Tom who's going to do my hair because it's my WEDDING DAY!"

You could have heard a fly sneeze. The reception room grew still, and all the patrons leaned in to catch the drama. After quickly clearing her throat, Connie conducted a rather animated, but hushed, phone conversation with Maurice, the salon owner.

Maurice instantly appeared from the back room like a genie released from a bottle. He hurried me out of the jam-packed reception room in triple step, then taking one look at me, squealed in a high-pitched voice, "We must remain calm!" Then Maurice escorted me to a manicure station and instructed me to take a seat, saying, "Jasmine[1] will be here shortly to do your nails." With drama punctuating every word, he added, "Meanwhile, I'll try to squeeze you into my crowded schedule. Yes I, *Maurice*, will do your hair personally." Maurice spoke his own name with reverence, as if he were God's gift to the styling profession.

My composure began to slip at this point, but I made a valiant attempt at self-control and said simply, "Maurice, I'm sure you are a fine stylist—maybe even the best in the free world. However, this is my wedding day. And I must have *Tommm!*" By now my voice resembled the whining cry of Lucy Ricardo. Maurice narrowed his eyes, lowered his chin, offered a terse smile, clicked his heels, and spun around in a huff.

[1] Names have been changed.

"Now I've done it," I whimpered to Jasmine. "Before this day is over I'll probably have to resort to paying a gardener to snip around my head with lawn shears."

My stomach began to churn. While Jasmine pushed and poked my cuticles, the smell of polish remover had a dizzying effect on my already traumatized head. Connie spoke to me soothingly as she patted my hand and placed a wet towel on my forehead. "There, there now. We've located Tom. He's sorry about forgetting to mention his relocation. As soon as your nails and toes are finished, you may go directly to Tom's new shop; he's only three blocks away." Surely a happier woman had never drawn breath. I hugged Connie, grabbed my veil, and clip-clopped out of the salon in rubber thongs.

By now the snow had drifted into mounds. I found myself on slippery thong skis, sliding down icy little slopes. I crashed into my car door and gingerly fumbled with the key, hoping to avoid smearing my nail polish. When I spied Tom's new salon I cruised by it twice, scouting for a parking spot that would *not* require a repeat ski performance. No such luck. As I stepped from my car, I teetered at the top of a snowbank, snow plowing as best I could in my flip-flops, but finally landing with a thump—yes, on my rump—in full view of every customer in the salon.

Embarrassing myself in front of beauty parlor patrons was becoming habitual. I dusted snow from my crumpled veil and from my backside. Tom met me at the door. At first, he looked like a man who'd just been caught cheating on his wife, full of remorse and hoping for forgiveness. Once assured I was not angry, just grateful, his demeanor changed. He took my arm and led me to the shampoo chair like a gentle, expectant father escorting his pregnant wife into the hospital delivery room. Praise the Lord, and alleluia! I was in safe hands. As expected, Tom delivered and my hair looked great.

I dashed from the salon and scurried straight to the church, grateful the worst of my fears were behind me. But when I reached the bride's dressing room, I faintly heard Dad muttering to Larry's best man as they walked down the hall. "It won't be long now," Dad said, with a chuckle. "It's almost time for my speech."

Oh no, I gasped, *not that crazy father-of-the- bride speech-thing again.* In a panic, my thoughts raced to our wedding rehearsal the night before. Our pastor, Dr. Bob, had motioned my father to the front and issued instructions: "At this point I will say, 'Who gives this woman in marriage?' and that will be the signal for you to come forward and simply say, 'I do.'"

Dad, in his traditionally cocky manner, replied, "Oh, I'll have a lot more to say than that tomorrow."

Lord, I pleaded, *please don't let him turn this sacred moment into a circus!* Determined to push all unwelcome images from my mind, I made my final preparations for the short walk that would change my life. With the satin folds of my train perfectly in place, I raised my hand to make a slight, final adjustment to my veil. I smiled, brushed a speck of lint from the lapel of my father's tuxedo, and slipped my arm into his, preparing to enter the chapel.

"You sure are ugly, Mouse," Dad said with a grin. He could never quite bring himself to deliver a straightforward compliment. Most of the really sweet thoughts Dad had concerning me, I heard via his friends. For more than thirty years I hadn't realized my father was proud of me, until his best friend, Bill, told me how much I meant to Dad.

Arm in arm we started down the aisle. The beauty of the gathering took my breath away. I was in heaven, right up to the point when Dr. Bob said, "Who gives this woman in marriage?" I braced for a stream of wild, unruly words that would surely make up Dad's impromptu speech.

My father came forward, and after a long look into my eyes, placed my hand in Larry's. Dad's mouth opened as if to speak, but his voice simply . . . evaporated. Instead, a mist gathered in his eyes, and with a single blink, tears trickled down my father's cheeks. Dad patted my hand, then quietly, slowly took his seat.

On my wedding day I saw two things, both rare and sacred: I saw my Dad speechless, and I saw him weep. And in that moment I learned what I had longed to know all my life; my father's love, after all, was too deep for words.

Nougat Center

Every good thing bestowed and every
perfect gift is from above, coming down
[through earthly fathers]
from the Father of lights . . .

(James 1:17, paraphrase added)

The Truffle
with Cookies

*I*t was our first Christmas as a new family, Larry, Elizabeth, and me. A stressful year it was, too, as we all made the necessary adjustments to blend ourselves together. Larry and I juggled careers and travel schedules, but nine-year-old Elizabeth had the real challenge, coping with a new school, new friends, and hardest of all, a new mom! I wanted our first Christmas to be *perfect*.

So we began with a snowy day at the tree farm scouting the perfect, twelve-foot blue spruce. But once our tree was perfectly decorated, it developed a perfectly nasty habit of falling squarely into the middle of our coffee table. Larry ultimately secured it by placing a nearly perfect fifty-pound toolbox on one leg of the perfect tree stand, which made a lovely bulge underneath the perfect Christmas tree skirt. Then we drank perfect eggnog before our perfect fire to celebrate this perfectly *awful* tree experience.

The next day a trip to the mailbox revived my holiday spirits when I discovered a cookie party invitation—ladies only, of course. This was the first party invitation we'd received since moving to Lawrence, Kansas, and it sounded like the best way for me to meet our neighbors, and join mainstream motherhood.

The invitation instructed each woman to bake twenty-four dozen cookies and submit her recipe to avoid duplications. After the party we would each take home twenty-four dozen different kinds of cookies, and have a full freezer for the holidays.

It sounded harmless enough. I could do this. I found a recipe that sounded scrumptious, and RSVP'd. Then the nightmare began. Now I must tell you, before this party invitation came, the only cookies I had ever baked in my entire life were sliced from a roll. But I knew I couldn't fail. This recipe had all the best ingredients: peanut butter, chocolate *and* butterscotch chips, plus nuts. How could this be anything but perfectly wonderful!

After dinner, the night before the party, I put a Christmas CD on the stereo, dressed Elizabeth and myself in matching aprons, and fired up the Cuisinart (hoping to impress my new daughter with my motherly baking talents). In went the peanut butter, on went the switch, whirrrr went the motor, and then it started to smoke. Things rolled downhill fast.

The Cuisinart destroyed, I began to hand mix ingredients at a fevered pace. By midnight I'd proudly baked ten dozen cookies—only fourteen more to go. My family, having tasted the first batch, assured me these were the *worst cookies ever baked*, and trudged off to bed. Indignant, I tasted one myself. The label "worst cookies ever baked" had been a clear understatement. These were not cookies to die for—these were cookies to die from! I panicked, but baked on . . . faster, faster. I just wanted this nightmare to end.

Ohhh, but it was only beginning! Hours later, the baking completed, I packaged each dozen cookies into Baggies. Then after scrounging up a Tupperware container suitable for transporting cookies to neighborhood parties, I collapsed, exhausted, into bed. Within moments, the alarm annoyed me from my sleep. I put on my best jean skirt, gathered my Tupperware, and headed out the door.

At the end of my driveway I spied my neighbor. She waved and flashed a cheery smile as she walked. I couldn't help comparing my jean skirt with her outfit: a beautiful, long skirt with matching Christmas sweater, and a necklace of Christmas tree lightbulbs that flashed off and on.

The outfit was intimidating enough, with me in my dress denim, but what she carried *terrified* me. Over her arm hung a sterling silver basket decorated with holly and ivy. Safely tucked inside, as though she were transporting the Hope diamond, were her twenty-four dozen cookies.

A *showoff,* I told myself. Surely the other women would be more casual. After all, this was a party, not a contest. Right?

Arriving at the party, our hostess greeted me in a Christmas dress even more stunning than my flashing neighbor's. A quick glance round the room revealed I was the only guest lacking the proper festive attire. Then I noticed the dining room. The table was the very picture of Currier & Ives, a plethora of divine baskets decorated with spectacular red-and-gold bows, angels, and old-world Santa Clauses. In each one nestled price-less cookies; these had been baked, no doubt, from recipes which traveled to this country on the Mayflower!

The cookies themselves were creatively wrapped and tied with beautiful ribbons, and tiny pinecones or jingle bells. Each cookie boasted tastebud euphoria! Mine were boasting Pepto Bismol, and looking more like chicken nuggets—extra crispy!

The hostess kindly escorted me to the kitchen, where guests were sipping hazelnut coffee, and graciously asked if I'd like to borrow a silver tray on which to arrange my *Baggies!* I gratefully accepted.

I found myself mumbling pathetic excuses for my appearance and my baking. Then a brilliant idea flashed across my mind, *I'll shift the focus from me to our children.* I quickly learned these professionals were all up on the latest parenting books and techniques, while I was only beginning my role as stepmother. I hadn't even discovered the parenting section of the library yet.

Soon realizing that I was a bomb at chitchat, I bravely attempted some humor. Each quip dangled painfully from the tip of my tongue, then fell flat on the Italian tile floor. Even my wit had failed me. Now came the hard truth. Here I was, the briefcase-toting frequent flier, who had entertained clients in fine restaurants all across the country, having to admit I was too inept to function socially at a simple, neighborhood cookie party.

Soon it came time for the party highlight and ultimate embarrassment—sampling the cookies. I winced each time a guest came near my cookies, praying she would choose another more tasty batch. Mercifully, I think the Baggies fended off a few, but to my dismay, one poor soul popped one in her mouth.

I have to hand it to her; she smiled and tried not to look shocked as she chewed. She was, of course, far too polite to place the horrid bite in her napkin, though heaven knows she wanted to. The rest of the room chatted and munched on, while my eyes glazed over. I slumped in the corner, numb from embarrassment. Finally *thank yous* and *good-byes* were being said. I left the party a changed woman, with a new appreciation for stay-at-home moms.

During the lonely walk home, tears splattered my Tupperware. *Lord, I'm such a failure at this mother thing,* I whimpered silently. *I can't even bake a decent cookie. I felt like a leper at that party. I wanted a perfect Christmas, but I've made a perfect mess!* I didn't hear an audible response, but pouring out my heart to the Lord was as soothing as the aloe I'd rubbed on my burned baking fingers. Then I remembered something magnificent—Jesus loved lepers.

By the time I reached my own front door and turned the key, Larry was home from his Saturday morning errands. He greeted me with a happy "Hi, how was the party, Hon?" My silence and sad eyes spoke the awful truth.

Just then Elizabeth flew down the stairs. "Wow, look at all these cookies. Let's eat 'em." Larry's arm slipped around my waist. "I know this wasn't easy, and I'm very proud of you." A word fitly spoken. God reminded me He didn't expect perfection—and neither did my family.

I gratefully took this revelation as a freshly baked truffle from heaven and tossed the last of the worst cookies ever baked in the can. Sure, I'd failed in Betty Crocker's eyes, but the eyes that really count saw the heart of the baker. And still loved her.

Nougat Center

There is therefore now no condemnation
for those who cannot bake.
For the law of the Spirit . . .
set me free from the law
of baking perfection. Alleluia!

(Rom. 8:1-2 paraphrased)

Truffled Feathers

I am captivated. Sitting in the serenity of the sanctuary, I scribble notes as the Bible study teacher describes some fascinating, God-inspired behavior. The courageous acts he speaks about were not performed by King David, the Apostle Paul, or even Christ. They were accomplished by eagles.

As a weaver weaves angora yarn, the gifted teacher intertwines biblical truths with the mysteries of the animal kingdom.

"When an eagle finds himself in a thunderstorm," he explains, "he doesn't cower in his nest like other birds do. At the approach of bad weather, he instinctively heads for higher ground, even a mountaintop. When the worst of the storm is on him, the eagle braces himself. He faces it head-on throwing out his breast, fully extending his wings, and inviting the storm to take its best shot." *Wow,* I think, *face the storm head-on.*

The teacher continues his intriguing description. "The moment that wind sweeps across the bird's broad wings, the storm itself sends the eagle soaring like a rocket, up, over the top of the clouds, into the calm air above the swirling gale. He hovers. When the storm passes, the great, majestic bird glides softly, safely back to earth."

Though my body's still sitting in the church pew, my mind is soaring in the clouds with eagles. I have to admit the eagle's courage stands in sharp contrast to my typical nest-hugging behavior. *I often feel like a birdbrain,* I think with a grin, *but I'm a far cry from being eagle-minded.* There are many things I'd rather not face. I do not know, as I mull over this rich metaphor from nature, that one day an eagle will be my lifeline.

Opening to the book of Deuteronomy, the teacher reads, "Like an eagle that stirs up its nest, that flutters over its young, spreading out its wings, catching them, bearing them on its pinions" (Deut. 32:11 RSV). *So the Lord cares for me,* I whisper in self-assurance.

"Like a wise human parent," the speaker explains, "a mama eagle encourages her eaglets to leave the nest on their own. But if met with reluctance, she employs a mother bird's version of tough love. Flying high above the nest where the baby roams, content and unaware, mama will suddenly swoop down upon her young. She offers no more warning than a loud screech, striking from behind and knocking the unsuspecting little guy right out of the nest.

"The terrified baby flaps for its life. Meanwhile, the mother hovers alongside, calling tenderly as a continual reminder—the eaglet is not alone. If the little guy panics, he'll soon lose his balance and spin out of control, screeching as beak and tail feathers whirl in a blur."

I was enormously relieved when the teacher went on to share that the mama eagle will not fly idly by. At the critical point in the free fall, Mother swoops in and supports the offspring with her strong wings. Mama eagle permits him to rest on her shoulders just long enough to regain his balance, then quickly drops out from under him. Again the air will fill the baby's little wings. Again he may panic and fall. Again she will call out in reassurance or glide under him with temporary support as before, all the while encouraging him toward his next attempt. The mother eagle repeats the pattern, never tiring of the process, building her baby's trust and confidence one day at a time. *Just as You, Lord, teach me, strengthen me, reassure me, and catch me.*

"Then," the teacher slows his voice for emphasis, "in one magnificent moment, the eaglet soars."

ॐ

Not long after that eagle lesson, I would be pushed from my nest, heading for free fall. I'll never forget that fateful evening when I stood at the kitchen counter, mashing hamburger, bread crumbs, and spices into meatloaf, while Elizabeth practiced spelling words at the kitchen table. It was a month before Christmas 1992, and over the living room stereo the angels were heralding "Joy to the World." Then Larry came home from work.

"Hi, handsome," I chirped.

He smiled weakly, barely brushing my cheek with an absentminded kiss. I followed instinctively, bracing myself for bad news. The angel voices ground to a screeching halt as my husband's words hit me like a lead fruitcake.

"We've been transferred to Dallas."

Can't be, I thought. *Unthinkable.* Larry babbled something about being sorry. I only caught bits of his lament.

"I know the timing is awful. I know your dad is sick, that you promised to drive him to his cancer treatments." But I couldn't hear him clearly through the terrible ripping sounds of my world coming apart at the seams. "Honey," Larry bravely concluded, "let's look on the bright side."

"There is no bright side," I cried. "My father may die. I'm needed here. I promised to be with him, no matter what."

That night, as I wiped away tears in the darkness, I prayed silently, *God, I know You would never do this to us. You'll fix it somehow; I know You will.*

Buzzing down the Kansas turnpike two weeks later, heading to a business appointment, I had to accept the unthinkable. God had not *fixed it,* the move was on. I was close to panic; my own beak and tail feathers now whirled in a blur. As I drove along, my mind was stuck in cruise control, fixed on morbid thoughts of endless gloom.

Suddenly, I was aware of being in close proximity to an eagle habitat. The beautiful birds nested near the river in Lawrence, Kansas, where the fishing was good. I'd promised myself for several years that I would visit the majestic creatures. Now it was too late. One more promise broken, one more dream unfulfilled.

I'd been making a long, growing, mental list of things I'd miss about home: Dad, my in-laws, lifetime friendships, the brilliant orange and gold oak leaves in October. Treasures I'd once accepted so casually. Now the thought of not having them left me in agony.

Depression stuck to me, as Mom used to say, like a new best friend. I almost welcomed it, believing a morose friend would be better than no friend at all—which is what I expected to have in Texas. Since desperate times call for desperate prayers, this day as I drove along the turnpike I prayed, *Lord, as a special farewell Christmas present, could I please see an eagle? Just one? If I could see an eagle soaring, I would know You are here beside me in this free fall. You would help me hold out my wings as I face this coming storm.* Miles passed, and I had all but given up, when I saw him out of the corner of my eye. Not the bird I'd asked for, but the truffle God knew I needed. A van with a big, green,

ridiculous eagle painted on its side pulled next to
my car and proceeded to accompany me home,
like a lonely stray that would not leave.

For miles, the silly, green bird was never out of
my sight. The longer I drove, the more tickled I got
until finally I burst out with a soul-cleansing laugh,
saying, "Lord, You are too much." I felt I was sharing a good laugh with a dear friend.

On the first day of the new year, just after
midnight, we rolled into Dallas. I was asleep, feeling far from home, far from eagles, and even more
distant from God. But when we hit the city limits, a
divine hand must have jostled me awake. I wiped
the sleep from my eyes just in time to see God's
welcome mat—a billboard sporting a picture of a
giant eagle. I could almost hear God chuckle, "I'm
God in Texas, too, you know." I laughed out loud,
thanking God for His sense of humor, and for
restoring mine.

Nougat Center

Yet those who wait for the Lord
Will gain new strength;
They will mount up
with wings like eagles,
They will run and not get tired,
They will walk and not become weary.
[They will move and not feel
abandoned!]

(Isa. 40:31, paraphrase added)

Key Lime Truffles

*I*t's hard to keep the faith when circumstances are screaming, "God's forgotten you!" But even in the midst of deep pain, God is there in the darkness calling, "I'm here. I love you." I've never been more amazed at His ability to reach into my crumbling world with tenderness than in the summer of 1992.

I ran for the phone, dreading at the same time the news I might hear. Daddy's voice quavered as he forced himself to press out the words, "The report is bad, Mouse. The doctor wants to remove the whole bladder; the tumor's malignant."

"I'll be right there, Dad."

I was terrified. I'd lost Mom what seemed like only moments ago. Now this. I knew my fear would probably be visible to Dad and my step-mother,

Gerry. For all our sakes, I had to pull myself together. Good cheer was in order, but I was fresh out. Grasping for any straw, I decided to stop by my favorite yogurt store, unconsciously I'm sure, searching for a bit of comfort in a cup. I whispered a prayer as I drove, but my mind was in a muddle of worry. And yet, it's odd what thoughts come shooting through our brains in times of stress.

"Lord," I found myself saying aloud, "I sure would love some key lime yogurt today." It was sort of a P.S. to my prayer, a rabbit-trail thought.

Now true yogurt connoisseurs know that key lime is a rarely offered flavor. With the overwhelming crisis facing my dad right then, a prayer about yogurt seemed embarrassingly shallow. So I closed my prayer with an apology. "Lord, I'm sorry for making such a ridiculous request in light of all the really big things we need help with right now."

Walking through the door of the yogurt shop, I searched the flavor board and suddenly smiled. The black-and-white tile of the yogurt store had become holy ground. A knowing grin I save only for God crossed my face as I placed my order for the flavor of the day: key lime. In honor of a new peace within, I ordered an extra-large cone, savoring every limey lick.

⁂

I made small talk in the waiting room with Gerry on the day of Dad's bladder surgery, chatting breezily, as if by the tone of my voice I could make it all better. We both looked up anxiously at the doctor who joined us much too soon to be bearing good news.

"The cancer was further along than we'd hoped. Taking the bladder would not help him now; we decided to leave it, to help him maintain his dignity during the time he has left."

⁂

We celebrated Christmas in the hospital that year, with Dad in and out of consciousness. We all knew this would be his last holiday with us as we sat on the sterile, orange plastic chairs in the waiting room of St. Luke's hospital. No tree, no turkey, no home-fire burning.

The fragile strings of my heart were snapping one by one as I stood helpless vigil over my father. I agonized when panic gripped Dad, and flinched when he grabbed the cords of plastic tubing that tethered him to this earth. With superhuman strength for his ninety-eight pounds, he didn't merely yank the tubes from his arm, he snapped them in two.

Restraining straps came next. *Please don't tie down his hands. . . . He's a dentist. . . . His hands are precious to him. . . . He would never even use them to hammer a nail!* I screamed silently to myself.

Gerry and I slept in chairs pushed together by Dad's bed, when we slept at all. We ate poorly, cried frequently, prayed constantly, but mostly we waited. I dreaded the hours to come.

One thing was painfully clear, Dad was waiting too. Waiting for someone to summon the courage to tell him, "It's okay to die, Dad; let go and let God take it from here. You're leaving us in good hands."

How can a wife whisper those words to her God-given companion? How can she plunge herself willingly into grief unimaginable? And how can an only child speak of death to her last living parent? Who possessed the courage for such a task? My answer, "Not me, Lord."

About eight one evening I grew restless. Deciding that Gerry and I could use a pick-me-up, I wandered down to the hospital cafeteria. *Maybe some ice cream would taste good*, I thought. Opening the freezer door, the God-grin crossed my lips once more, and tears welled up in my eyes. The entire freezer was filled to the brim—with key lime yogurt.

Each trip from Dad's hospital room to the freezer and back, over the next five days, increased my faith. Each evening, God spoke to me through the limey refreshment in the Styrofoam cup that I was not alone—and neither was Dad. No matter the hell inside the hospital, heaven awaited beyond the ceiling tiles. Death would not triumph here!

Dad's last moments were just as they should have been. Alone with him, I softly stroked his beautiful, thick, salt-and-pepper hair, and finally the words I prayed for just tumbled from my mouth. "Jesus will be here soon, Daddy," I began softly. "When He comes, you go with Him. It's okay. We'll be fine. Let go and rest." I kissed his head for the final time; it was a sweet kiss.

Nougat Center

*Even though I walk through the valley
of the shadow of death,
I fear no evil; for Thou art with me;
Thy rod and Thy staff [and Thy
yogurt], they comfort me.*

(Ps. 23:4, paraphrase added)

Friendship Truffles

*E*ver had a time, maybe even a few years, where you felt stuck on a treadmill of tragedy? Believe me, I understand. I suffered so many losses in a five-year time span that I began to lose count.

First came my mother's unexpected death during routine surgery. Soon after, my nine-year career ended abruptly, followed by my dad's lost battle with cancer, and my favorite uncle's death just six months later. On top of it all came the big move. Too much gone much too soon.

In four decades, I'd never lived farther than an hour from the little house where I grew up in Kansas City, Missouri. To move away from all I'd known was excruciating. Not only had I lost parents, job, and home in what seemed like one extended, grief-laden moment, I was now losing a big part of my identity. With the slamming of the American Van Lines doors, the relocation was final, and a very long, very comfortable chapter of my life was left behind.

Now in Texas, my stress-o-meter was off the charts, and my former life seemed light-years away. In this strange, new city I knew no one—and no one knew me. I was like an amnesia victim, a woman with no history. I felt as if the last forty years of my life were irrelevant. In the six months since the move, I'd made precious few acquaintances, and no real friends. One morning, frustration over my powerlessness to change the situation sent me over the edge.

I was sitting at a major intersection. An ordinary day in every way, except the traffic light was malfunctioning. A uniformed officer directing the traffic motioned for me to stop. I did. The driver behind me didn't. I immediately looked in my rearview mirror and saw two teenage boys snickering and pointing. In this one moment, five years of anger and frustration erupted with the fury of Mount St. Helen's. I leaped from my car, yelling as I went, literally hopping up and down, demanding the policeman come immediately and drag these hoodlums to jail.

"What seems to be the trouble here, Ma'am?" he asked.

"Trouble!" I exploded. "I stopped just as *you* directed me to do, and these juvenile delinquents deliberately hit my car." Taking the officer by the arm, I attempted to drag him toward the perpetrators, screaming as I went. "I want you to make an example of these future felons!"

The calm officer very gently guided me back into my car, patted me on the shoulder, and said, "You go on home, now, little lady. I'll handle this one by myself."

"What in the world are you doing, Kali?" I stammered, "You're cracking up."

As I drove toward home, I tried to collect my scattered thoughts, continuing to dialogue with myself. (Who else did I have to talk to? It was pitiful.)

"Maybe I should check out that Tuesday morning Bible study at church. It might help me focus in the right direction—or at the very least, keep me out of jail!"

Soon I was a regular member of the Tuesday class. Studying the Scripture with these women was like a shot of helium into the balloon of my rapidly deflating sanity. My spirits began to rise slowly, but I was still very aware that I was a relative stranger among the native clan, and my instincts told me this was not the place to unburden my sorrows. And then, the *phenomenon* occurred.

During our class, it was the custom for each person to take a turn reading Scripture aloud. When my turn came, I broke down in tears as I read, "I will lift up my eyes to the mountains; From whence shall my help come? My help comes from the Lord" (Ps. 121:1-2). I didn't even know why I was crying. I only knew I couldn't stop.

I was never quite sure whether the ladies' silent response to my tears was motivated by grace, sympathy, or awkwardness, but they never commented on my odd behavior. Wordlessly, week after week, a Kleenex box would simply slide in my direction.

Each Tuesday was the same—I dissolved into tears as I read the Scriptures aloud and inwardly died from embarrassment. "What I need is a hug," I told the Lord, "just one friend to hug me."

The harder I tried to control my emotions, the more I choked up. Humiliated, I considered quitting the Bible study. But the part of me that was fighting for emotional survival dared take a risk, so I invited a woman named Penny to lunch. I barely knew her, but to my delight she accepted. Over a grilled veggie pizza, I shared my embarrassing predicament: the grief, the tears, and the angry flare-ups. We began lunch as acquaintances; we left, after a meal and two cups of coffee, as friends. Somewhere between the mushrooms and the eggplant, a spiritual bond was formed.

We discussed my uncontrollable weeping, and Penny came up with a beautiful thought, "Maybe, Kali, your tears are an involuntary response to your total reliance on God during this time of grief." I stopped chewing. Penny had my full attention.

She probed further, "Kali, could it be that your old sources were removed so God could reveal Himself as your truest and best Comforter? And now when you read from His Word, the intimacy of the situation completely overcomes you? If you are leaning on God more fully than ever, the Scriptures have probably taken on a deep, personal meaning, tapping into the reality of God's tenderness as He touches your heart. It brings forth tears that need to be cried."

Now why didn't I think of that? This woman was brilliant!

Later that evening, I relaxed into a comfy chair at home as I thought over the day—the fun I'd had with Penny, the delight of being heard, understood, and comforted by the insight of a real live person! I thought, *God is like bread, the sustainer of my life. And everything else is gravy.*

Precious Father, thank You for today's portion of bread—the assurance of Your presence. But I have to tell You, I'm especially grateful for today's ladle of gravy—in the form of one human friend.

Nougat Center

Do not fear,
for I am with you;
Do not anxiously look about you,
for I am your God.
I will strengthen you,
surely I will help you.

(Isa. 41:10)

Penny Candy or Truffle Treasure?

*A*uthor Frederick Buechner tells of a time he was parked by the road, terribly worried and depressed over his daughter's illness. As a minister he undoubtedly knew God cared about his situation, but in tough times even strong faith may waiver. Suddenly aware of a car speeding by, he looked up just in time to see the license plate. A single word was printed on that plate: TRUST. "What do you call a moment like that?" asks Buechner. Was it a word from God, a joke of life, or both?

Later, he learned the owner of the plate was a trust officer in a bank. Having read the story about the incident, the banker looked Buechner up and gave him the plate. Buechner writes, "It is rusty around the edges and a little battered, and it is also as holy a relic as I have ever seen." Call them holy relics or tangible truffles, they offer needed reminders of God's presence. Are there any such relics around your house, little tokens of God's affection saved during a tough time?

My friend Jackie beams whenever she sees a morning glory. Before I knew these flowers held any special significance, I gave Jackie a ceramic butter dish decorated with morning glories as a birthday gift, and watched in utter astonishment as she burst into tears, exclaiming repeatedly, "It's just too wonderful." I probed a bit, only to learn I had stumbled upon a sacred icon.

While recovering from the shock of an airplane accident that killed her husband of twenty-nine years, Jackie sought comfort in the seclusion of a little cabin in the woods. After a day and night of tears and prayers, Jackie woke early and went to the porch to sip coffee and watch the sun rise.

She was overwhelmed by the vision that greeted her. The fence line that bordered the cabin extended for several miles, and as far as Jackie could see, the fence was covered with thousands of sky blue morning glories in full bloom. In that instant, Jackie's spirit began its long, slow healing process. And to this day, Jackie's spirit soars whenever she sees a morning glory.

I have a few holy relics of my own, but my favorite is a penny. One single penny. It came from God's hand into my real world with a familiar but powerful message—"In God We Trust"—and I am always reminded to do just that.

Shortly after settling into my new church home in Dallas and joining the Bible study, I received a call from a woman inviting me to serve on a church board called the women's council. Not much of a joiner, but anxious to make new friends, I agreed. The women were planning a spring luncheon, and my assignment was to locate a speaker. *What?* I thought. *I've only been in Dallas long enough to find my toothbrush. How am I supposed to find a speaker?* Then came the clincher: these women had no money budgeted for a speaker. They expected an afternoon of rich inspiration—for free!

I crawled into bed that night completely overwhelmed. "This is too much," I grumbled to the Lord. "I can't possibly handle this by myself. Please help me."

In the early morning around 3:00 A.M., a ferocious thunderstorm hit Dallas. A tooth-rattling boom awakened me so abruptly I thought the kitchen had exploded. I found myself standing bolt upright beside my bed. My Rip-van-Winkle husband was oblivious to the disaster. (I have no idea how he does this. Even with earplugs on, I could hear a pine needle hit a snowbank.)

Our bedroom was now flooded with light, and though not quite wide awake, I dashed through the house fully expecting to see it burning down around us. Something was very odd. All was calm—yet all was bright! *So what's up with the glow?* I wondered, as I walked toward the window and raised the blind. Then, I discovered the source of all the commotion. Lightning had hit the oak tree in the backyard. That explained the boom. But the light, why did the light seem to linger in the bedroom?

Was this some sort of contemporary version of the burning bush? I mumbled to myself, quite confused, but dazzled. Wide awake and still a bit unsettled, I tried unsuccessfully to go back to sleep. I've never quite grasped the "sheep-counting" concept, so I tried counting my blessings instead. Realizing I hadn't said many prayers of gratitude since our move to Texas, it felt good to simply say thanks—

especially for the small stuff. Then my thoughts suddenly went from ordinary to extraordinary. As I prayed, unusual visual images began to form in my mind. I saw myself dropping pennies around my church. Pennies in the parking lot, pennies in the choir loft, pennies in the sanctuary. *What's this about, Lord?* I wondered, even as the images kept coming. Next I saw the fellowship hall where the luncheon was to be held. The decorations seemed a bit bizarre: black tablecloths with three balloons on each table, two black and one copper, tethered (by copper ribbons) to a roll of pennies.

The most unsettling visual image was the podium, for behind it stood none other than me. It was almost like watching a movie in simultaneous fast forward and slow motion. Over the next few hours, until dawn broke, I scribbled down words I felt the Lord prompting me to share. I've never heard an audible voice when God speaks to me, maybe you have. But the voice I sometimes hear within my spirit is more compelling than any audible voice, and this was one of those times.

God impressed me with the concern that His children often take daily blessings for granted, stepping over them the way some people walk by pennies in parking lots. In addition, I felt nudged to share all He'd done to help me get over life's humps. Though I'd once felt trials were pure torment, I was realizing that even during the saddest moments, God would be there to comfort and encourage. Through my darkness, I'd come to know light. And that light was meant to be shared.

That lightning bolt was my wake-up call. Call it a vision, a purpose, a mission, God had a message for the luncheon: "You are never alone, even when the storms of life shake you awake in the middle of the night." I called the speech "Pennies from Heaven" and believe to this day that the title was a gift from above. But my initial reaction was much like the nervous orator Moses. "Not me, Lord. I can't speak publicly about such intimate things. I'm gonna have to share a pew with these women on Sundays. If I'm a total flop, I'll not only embarrass You and me, I'll have to leave and start over in another church."

I was plagued by doubts. "Lord, those women don't want to hear about my personal little dramas. Some of that stuff is a real downer. People want a light, upbeat kind of affair."

But God continued to press, "Haven't you been scared before? Didn't I give you what you needed most, when you most needed it? Others are hurting just as you hurt, Kali. But they don't know I'm with them, as you have come to understand. I want you to remind My daughters that I'm here for them, by sharing what I have done for you."

"Well, they won't believe me, Lord," I argued back. "They'll think I'm arrogant, suggesting I see things they miss."

"Then don't be arrogant," the Lord countered. "Be loving—and leave their believing to Me."

Ever argue with God like this? It's peculiar how we are often given moments of great inspiration, only to be followed by moments of great reservation. Doubts arrive to snatch away our joy or leave us in a misty-minded fog, trying to sort out what's God, and what's our own invention. The old, "Is this God, or indigestion from last night's pizza?" dilemma.

Unable to gain peace, I simply had to know. All doubts must go. I summoned as much faith as my timid soul could muster, and spoke boldly. "Lord, if this really is something You want me to do, and not just my own panic attack over finding a speaker, I

need some sort of sign." There. I had tossed the ball back in His court. Good night.

The next day as I pulled into the parking lot for the Prestonwood Newcomer's luncheon, I was grateful my friend Carolyn would be meeting me there. During lunch I told her about my strange sleepless night. Hoping I would make *some* sense I confided, "Carolyn, I think God wants me to tell stories about my own life. He wants me to share the details of His comfort and help when times were tough. And He wants me to use the illustration of pennies from heaven. What do you think of all this?"

Carolyn studied me awhile. "That's not for me to say, Kali. This is between you and God. Are you going to speak, or not?"

"Oh, I don't know. The whole idea scares me silly," I confessed. "I'm not too worried about having to make the speech, though, because I asked God, if this is of Him, to send me a confirmation." I laughed, "So far I haven't had a clear sign. No angels hovering with banners or anything."

In the middle of our conversation, a waiter cleared our dishes to serve dessert. As he lifted my bread plate, there, hiding under the plate, was a

single, shiny, copper penny. Carolyn sat open-mouthed.

"In God we trust," the tiny words read. It may as well have grown legs, put on dancing shoes, and shouted the encouragement. We both stared in stunned amazement at this most unexpected and holy relic. Carolyn found her voice first. "I don't know about you, Kali, but I've got goose bumps. If that's not a sign, I don't know what is!" I shook my head slowly as though the movement might help me grasp what just happened.

"Yes," I answered with deep conviction. "I not only have a sign, I have you as my witness, Carolyn. If I should ever doubt, and I'm sure some days I will, please promise to remind me of this." I was not alone, God was with me—and now Carolyn was too. Where two or more are gathered together, sometimes truffles come raining down in the most unexpected of ways. Like pennies from heaven.

Nougat Center

*This is a sign—[copper pennies]—
between Me and you throughout
your generations, that you may know
that I am the Lord who sanctifies you.*

(Ex. 31:13, paraphrase added)

Speaking of Truffles . . .

I keep forgetting, when exactly are you speaking at that luncheon, Kali?" asked Carolyn, referring to my commitment born of that strange night vision, several months earlier.

Carolyn smiled as she pulled a cookies 'n' cream ice-cream sandwich from the freezer and handed it to a hungry, impatient seventh grader. Once each month I met Carolyn in the cafeteria of Renner Middle School, where we sold ice cream for the PTO.

"Oh, Carolyn, the luncheon is less than a month away, and I'm getting *real* nervous."

As we discussed some of the stories I planned to share at the luncheon, I confessed, "I'm afraid my openness will threaten the women at church, and

they'll distance themselves from me after the speech. They might think I'm . . . well, weird."

Carolyn tossed me a sympathetic nod, as she made change for the ponytailed blond slurping on a Rainbow Pop. Just then something zipped between us, rolled beneath our selling table, finally coming to rest beside my purse. I bent down . . . another penny. I laughed and held up the little messenger of courage for Carolyn to see. Carolyn joked, "I don't believe this. You're starting to be too weird to hang out with, Kali."

Another truffle, to chase away today's doubts. Thank You, Lord, for the affirmation. I wrapped my fingers around the copper confirmation, and smiled toward heaven.

ॐ

In spite of God's consistent confirmation, on the actual day of the luncheon, my nerves and worries began churning again. Why couldn't I just get my full dose of peace once and for all? Why this daily need to keep bringing this fear to Him? I understood with new empathy why the number one fear on every survey turns out to be speaking in public. (The number two fear is death.)

D-day, the day of the speech, landed on April 29,

coinciding with the date of my birth. *What a way to spend a birthday—with your knees knocking, your palms sweating, and your hair graying with every tick of the clock!* Like an unexpected penny, a favorite verse of Scripture appeared in my thoughts. " 'And who knows whether you have not come to the kingdom for such a time as this?' " (Es. 4:14 RSV). Deep in my heart I wondered, *Has God's preparation in my life now led me to this moment—for this purpose?*

"I'll be back in time to kiss you good-bye," called my husband that morning, as he headed out the door to grab a bagel and a newspaper at the corner store.

"Okay, Hon, but I'll be leaving in thirty minutes." I waved at my husband, then resumed nervously applying finishing touches of makeup, wishing there was some sort of calming cream I could rub on my nerves.

As the official "countdown to luncheon" began, my anxiety reached its full crescendo. I sank into my prayer chair, but the beginnings of spiritual calm halted with the telephone's loud ring.

"Oh, Kali," said the distressed voice on the line, "I have terrible news. John Wood was found in his dorm last night, dead in his bed. Everyone at church is reeling from the shock! And Anne, the boy's mother, who was going to introduce you at the luncheon, will obviously be tending to family matters. She left for the college campus last night." [1]

The caller went on. "This blow has hit hard, Kali. I thought you should know the sad news before arriving at the church today. I didn't want you to be blindsided. So don't take it personally if folks seem distracted, or even unreceptive. . . ." I placed the receiver in its cradle and buried my face in my hands. The horror of every parent's worst nightmare had come true, and I cried a mother's tears.

"Oh, Lord," I cried, "I can't possibly speak to those shocked, grieving mothers. What will I say?"

Larry walked in the door carrying his bagel bag and newspaper. Humming a happy tune, he was totally unaware of the crushing phone call that had changed my complexion from rosy pink to ashen gray. I'm sure Larry misread my anguished expression as mere stage fright. Before I could share the awful news, Larry said cheerfully, "Kali, I don't understand this 'penny thing' you've got going with God, but I found something on top of the news stand. I think it belongs to you."

With a mischievous grin, Larry opened his hand

---

[1] Names have been changed.

and dropped a copper coin into my waiting palm. "Must be from Him," he said, the tone of his voice full of assurance.

"Not a doubt in my mind about that, Honey." I had no time to explain the phone call right then, so I simply kissed Larry, put the penny in my shoe, squared my shoulders, and headed out the door. I arrived early enough at the church to scatter my pennies undetected. During my speech, I planned to ask the question, "What did you do the last time you saw a penny on the ground?" I wanted to make sure the ladies passed by a few of them before coming into the luncheon, as sort of a pre-speech object lesson.

Then I entered the fellowship hall and discovered the women had carried on beautifully, in spite of their emotional pain. Black cloths draped the tables, and black and copper balloons bobbed on copper ribbons—just as I'd visualized that stormy night months before.

The churning sea in my aching stomach calmed the instant I rose to speak, as if the Lord had stopped my lurching nerves with the words, "Peace, be still." I spoke as if I'd been born for the moment.

"I know you are wondering about the decorations," I began, having overheard a few negative comments during our get-acquainted time. Many women thought our decorations were depressing, not at all the colors they'd have picked for a spring luncheon. No one, that is, except a wise God. I didn't even know the full reason God prompted me to choose such an unusual color combination until this moment. Suddenly, it was more than clear.

I explained, "The black cloths signify the down times in our lives, when circumstances are gloomy, and potential outcomes seem anything but bright. The black balloons represent thunderclouds, hovering on the horizon of a stormy day. But the single, copper balloon signifies a bright penny, shining in the midst of darkness."

At this point, I asked how many had seen pennies on their way into the luncheon room. Several hands went up. "How many of you picked one up?" I asked next. Very few hands were raised. "This is often the way it is with the small offerings of love and comfort that God sends us. They are there, but we step over them. Seeing only briefly or not at all, not taking them, not accepting them as our own personal gifts." I pointed to the roll of pennies in the center of one of the tables, then held one up in my hand. "This roll of pennies represents the wealth of God's unfailing presence in the center of our blackest moments. In other words, there are pennies of love all around us and plenty more in God's storehouse. God's supply is greater than all our need."

As I looked around the room, I thought of a line from "Amazing Grace": "I was blind, but now I see." I didn't understand before this moment, but now I saw. I saw that indeed, months before this day, God had cared enough about these women to speak through me to offer a bit of His comfort in this hour, on a day when our church body was in heart-wrenching pain.

"Thank You, Lord, for Your love and strength on this difficult day," I silently prayed as I gazed at the balloons tied to the penny rolls.

Nougat Center

I can do all things through Him
who strengthens me. . . .
And my God shall supply
all your needs according to His riches
in glory in Christ Jesus.

(Phil. 4:13, 19)

Truffled Reunion

Countless are the times when God has sent people to brighten my day or soften my way. But the sweetest of His blessings in my own life are moments when I'm allowed to be an instrument of God's grace, when *I become* a truffle from heaven.

Such was the occasion of my class reunion, and I'll never forget the mark it left on me. I had attended my five-year and fifteen-year reunions, and they were absolutely wonderful. Though we had 750 students in our graduating class at Oak Park High School, there were many close friendships within that large group. So many tearful good-byes were said at graduation, many vows made to stay in touch.

Though I had many close friends during high school, only two remain in contact today. They are among my dearest treasures. Ah, but at the reunion, the memories seemed to draw new breath, returning me to a past life and younger days.

Isn't it funny how years can pass with hardly a thought of a person, but a reunion brings back all the emotions surrounding your past encounters? As if suspended in freeze-frame, a conversation picks up, almost at the exact point where it trailed off years ago when we were standing by our lockers, wondering what college would be like. It was fun to see my classmates' hair—both guys and girls with long, straight, '60s hair now wore short, updated styles. And some seemed to have misplaced their hair entirely—or had purchased handy, hairy replacement patches. Some had married, some stayed single. Some divorced, some had not. Some had children, several had none.

Some people who once were friendly now greeted me with cool indifference—while many who treated me icily during school now warmed up a smidge. And, of course, the night held out the hope of romance: Old flames were rekindled, and at least one spark, I later heard, resulted in a marriage. It was a strange and wonderful evening when nothing had changed, and yet, everything had changed. I was totally lost in the magic of each moment, savoring every hug, delighting in every story, smile, and wave from across the room. Then Hal[1] walked in the door.

During high school, Hal was never a popular guy. He was greatly overweight, and shy, as I remember. But he always had a warm smile (and a complexion any girl would covet). Hal was one of the genuinely nice guys. I hadn't thought of Hal in fifteen years. Now here he was, heading my way, stylishly dressed, with that unforgettable smile. He looked fantastic, having lost at least eighty pounds. Obviously Hal had been working out with weights. Gesturing to a tall, handsome young man on his right, Hal said, "This is my son, Mark."

"Hal, I missed seeing you at the five-year reunion," I said, giving him a big hug.

"I wasn't ready yet," came the response.

"Ready, for what?" I asked.

His face grew uncharacteristically serious. "Kali, I never had a single good day in high school." I blinked, in disbelief.

"Marty McDonald made it his mission in life to make each day a living hell for me. He tormented and humiliated me constantly," Hal confessed. I

---

[1] Names have been changed.

was stunned. I never realized he was so unhappy. His smile had covered unseen pain.

He continued, "I always promised myself I would never go to a reunion until I was thin, and Marty was fat and bald." I raised my eyebrows, and Hal nodded toward a table in the back of the room. There sat Marty, a former muscle-bound member of our wrestling team. I had to admit, Marty looked more like the Pillsbury Doughboy than a star athlete. His thinning hair had an odd, contrived style as though he had let his eyebrows grow long, and then brushed them back over his head. Hal's wish had come true.

I asked Hal if seeing Marty in his present pudgy state was as great a moment as he had always imagined. "Nah," replied Hal. "I actually feel kind of sorry for him." As I said, Hal was genuinely nice.

Then Hal handed me a truffle, an affirmation so special I would cherish it forever. "You were always kind to me, Kali. You were one of those who made a difference. I always looked forward to seeing you in the halls, because I knew I could count on you to say 'Hi.' You didn't look past me as some others did; seeing you was often the high point of my day."

I choked down the huge lump in my throat, then

began digging frantically in my purse for a mint in an effort to divert my eyes, which were welling up with unexpected tears.

Though we can't always make the difference to everyone we see in this life, we can all make a difference for someone, in some small way. We can be God's compassion to a wounded woman, a lonely man, a hurting child. For someday, in eternity, a great reunion awaits us all. On that day we will, undoubtedly, come face-to-face with those we have cheered, and those we have jeered. May you discover, as I have, the everlasting joy when you are someone else's truffle from heaven.

Nougat Center

Thou didst awesome things which we [I] did not expect.

(Isa. 64:3)

If you have a comment or would like to share your own truffles with Kali Schnieders, please use the address below.

Or if you wish to schedule the author for a presentation to your company or organization, contact:

Truffles and Associates
17519 Oak Mount Place
Dallas, TX 75287

E-mail: KSTruffle@aol.com